# Musings Through Poetry

## Poorvi Rajak

**Anuragyam, New Delhi**

© Poorvi Rajak

This book has been published with all reasonable efforts taken to make the material error-free after the consent of the author. No part of this book shall be used, reproduced in any manner whatsoever without written permission from the author, except in the case of brief quotations embodied in critical articles and reviews.

The Author of this book is solely responsible and liable for its content including but not limited to the views, representations, descriptions, statements, information, opinions and references ["Content"]. The Content of this book shall not constitute or be construed or deemed to reflect the opinion or expression of the Publisher or Editor. Neither the Publisher nor Editor endorse or approve the Content of this book or guarantee the reliability, accuracy or completeness of the Content published herein and do not make any representations or warranties of any kind, express or implied, including but not limited to the implied warranties of merchantability, fitness for a particular purpose. The Publisher and Editor shall not be liable whatsoever for any errors, omissions, whether such errors or omissions result from negligence, accident, or any other cause or claims for loss or damages of any kind, including without limitation, indirect or consequential loss or damage arising out of use, inability to use, or about the reliability, accuracy or sufficiency of the information contained in this book.

Edition: January 2025
Publication: Anuragyam, New Delhi, India
Website: www.anuragyam.com
Email: editor@anuragyamgmail.com || +91-9999920037

MRP : Soft Cover    Rs. 200/-  ||  USD 15
          Hard Cover  Rs. 300/-  ||  USD 25

Cover Design: Er. Sachin Chaturvedi, Anuragyam
Illustration: Poorvi Rajak (Child Artist & Author)
Printing & Marketing by: Notion Press
Available in Anuragyam, Notion Press, Amazon, Flipkart
Distribution across India, USA, UK, Spain, Canada, France, Australia, Germany, Japan & 150+ countries

*I dedicate this little book*

*to the world*

# Asia Book of Records
## Presented to Poorvi Rajak

**Presented by**

# Shri M N Harendhira Prasad, IAS

Collector of Visakhapatnam district.
Andhra Pradesh

# Sri M. Venumohan
Chairman, Little Angels School, MVP Visakhapatnam

# Asia Book of Records
## Presented by
Right to Left: **Shri Kranti Kiran** (Director)
**Sri M. Venumohan** (Chairman)
**Smt. N. Indu Malini** (Principal)
**Smt. Rehana Shaik** (Class Counsellor)
Little Angels School, MVP Visakhapatnam

# Forewords

It is with immense pleasure and pride that I write this foreword for Poorvi Rajak's debut poetry collection, "Musings Through Poetry." As a fellow poet and admirer of the written word, I have been deeply moved and inspired by the depth, emotion and sheer artistry displayed in these verses. Poorvi's poetic voice is truly unique, blending a profound understanding of the human experience with a masterful command of language. Her poems traverse a wide range of themes, from the personal and introspective to the universal and societal, all the while maintaining a captivating and lyrical quality.

What strikes me most about Poorvi's work is her ability to capture the essence of emotions, whether it's the bittersweet nostalgia of lost innocence, the unwavering strength of the human spirit, or the awe-inspiring beauty of the natural world. Her words have a way of resonating deeply within the reader, leaving a lasting impression and a desire to revisit the poems time and again.

As a musical poet myself, I am particularly drawn to the rhythmic and melodic nature of Poorvi's writing. Her poems possess a musicality that seamlessly blends with the depth of their content, creating a harmonious and immersive experience for the reader. The way she weaves her words together is akin to a symphony, where each line and stanza flows effortlessly, creating a captivating and harmonious whole.

Through "Musings Through Poetry," Poorvi has not only showcased her exceptional talent as a poet but has also given voice to the universal experiences and emotions that connect us all. Her poems possess a rare and powerful combination of grace, grit and insight, inviting the reader to pause, reflect and see the world anew through her unique and imaginative lens.

This young author has written an amazing book of poetry. Each poem is well-written and inspiring. I highly recommend this book. We need more ambitious young people in this world. As a musical poet who has graced many stages, I find this book has motivated me to reinvent myself and strive to create better songs for the world. I humbly commend this remarkable collection of poems.

It is with great honour and enthusiasm that I recommend "Musings Through Poetry" to all lovers of poetry and literature. Poorvi Rajak is a rising star in the poetic firmament and I look forward to witnessing the continued evolution and impact of her remarkable talent.

*Jerome Bradley*
International Author, Writer and Poet
Musical Poet, New York, USA
Email: jeromebradley71@gmail.com

Address: No. 2-B, Nutech Narayana
Apartments, 48, Thirumalai Pillai Ln,
T Nagar, Chennai, Tamil Nadu – 600017
www.spacekidzindia.in

## Message

Sometimes the most extraordinary voices come from the youngest hearts. At thirteen, Poorvi Rajak from Visakhapatnam brings us a collection of poems that speaks with wisdom beyond her years. As a 9th-grade student at Little Angels School, she has already touched countless lives through her art, winning over 400 awards and setting multiple records.

But Poorvi is more than just her achievements. She's a young artist who paints with both brushes and words, who speaks on public stages with confidence and who moves with the discipline of a martial artist. Her previous books, available on Amazon and Flipkart, have already shown us glimpses of her creative spirit. Now, in this new collection, she shares more of her thoughts, dreams and observations about the world around her.

From winning the Asia Book of Records 2024 to earning recognition from ISRO, Poorvi has proven that age is just a number when it comes to creating beauty and inspiring others. Each poem in this collection carries the same dedication she brings to everything she does - whether she's competing in karate championships or speaking at national events.

As you read these poems, you'll discover the world through the eyes of a remarkable young girl who reminds us that creativity knows no bounds. Welcome to Poorvi's world of wonder, wisdom and words. Goodluck in all your endeavours dear Poorvi!!

Sincerely,

**Dr. Srimathy Kesan**
Founder, CEO, Space Kidz India

India Youth For Society
Model Plastic Recycling Project
GVMC Dumping Yard, Kapuluppada
Visakhapatnam 531163
support@plasticfreeindia.org
PH: 9703489797 WWW.IYFS.IN

## Message

India Youth For Society (IYFS), of which I am the Founder and President, organizes various activities such as painting, drawing and elocution competitions. Among the many participants, Poorvi Rajak stands out with her consistent participation in all our events. She never fails to win at least one prize, showcasing her remarkable talent and dedication. Her parents are always by her side and I have had the pleasure of interacting with them during our events. It was inspiring to learn about Poorvi's ambition of becoming a civil servant.

One day, I was pleasantly surprised when she presented me with a small book she had written. It was not long before her second book followed. Recently, I learned that she has written yet another book.

When she asked me to write a foreword for her latest work, I revisited her previous book, The Fascinating World of Poems. Many of her poems reflect her deep love for animals, her concern for Mother Earth and her passion for the nation. I truly admire her ability to express her thoughts and emotions through poetry. Her writing also captures her personal experiences, making her work relatable and insightful.

I wholeheartedly congratulate Poorvi on her continuous contributions to literature and encourage all students to read her books. Her journey is an inspiration for young minds to pursue their passions with dedication and creativity.

Sincerely,

**Appala Reddy Y**
President, India Youth For Society

# Message

Knowing Ms Poorvi Rajak with her nature of giftedness, intelligence, creativity, the brain, physical and cultural evolution and knowledge, skill and expertise I would say a Prodigy is here. Poetry is like a rollercoaster ride for our imagination, taking you on wild twists and turns through vast landscapes of emotions and ideas on a playground where words frolic, somersault and occasionally pull a trick on your unsuspecting mind for the universe of words, unlocking doors to new dimensions of expression and understanding.

Her third compilation "Musings of Poetry" with 75 more linguistic and poetic adventure is not just a few lines of fancy words but they explore the world of dormant creativity and allows one to dive deep into a window of imagination. She has pushed the boundaries in words, thoughts and the play of emotions.

Wishing Ms Poorvi Rajak more Poetic adventures and Pulitzer heights.

**Dr. Joe K. Kizhakudan**
Principal Scientist
Mariculture Division and HEAD of Regional Centre (HoRC) of
ICAR CMFRI, Visakhapatnam
Andhra Pradesh

# Message

It is with immense pride and joy that I extend my heartfelt congratulations to you, dear Poorvi, on the remarkable achievement of releasing your third book. Your journey as a multi-talented individual has been nothing short of extraordinary and it continues to inspire all of us. At Anuragyam, we take great pride in celebrating exceptional talent and you stand as a radiant example of dedication, passion and hard work. Your ability to excel in diverse endeavors is truly awe-inspiring. The release of your second book is not merely a milestone; it is a testament to your unwavering creativity, intellect and commitment to excellence. Your words hold a unique power to captivate, inspire and leave a lasting impact on readers. We are confident that this latest masterpiece will resonate as deeply as your first book did, earning the admiration and applause it rightfully deserves. May this new chapter in your literary journey bring you abundant success, recognition and fulfilment. Your accomplishments remind us all of the boundless potential of perseverance and passion. We at Anuragyam are deeply honored to have you as part of our community and eagerly look forward to witnessing the many milestones yet to come in your remarkable journey. Once again, congratulations on the release of your second book, Poorvi! May this achievement shine brightly as a beacon of your talent and determination.

*Sachin Chaturvedi*
Founder, Anuragyam

# Introduction

Around four years have passed since I have started writing poems. By now, I have written around 400 poems and 225 of them have been published in three separate books of mine, each containing 75 poems. This is my third book. This book holds even more poems which I have selected after much thought and consideration.

The poems in this book are all about all the deeply-rooted festivals we joyously celebrate and nature, which is integral for our survival on this planet. Most of the poems are about day-to-day situations in our lives which are seemingly mundane, but hold deep significance once we think about them. It is during those periods of deep thought and reflection when most of the poems were born. It is because of that that I decided to title this book "Musings through Poetry"

Poems just naturally kick in when I am in deep thought. It is impossible for me to think without poetry. Writing poems has improved my skill of expression and provided an outlet for my thoughts. Writing poems will forever remain one of my favourite ways to express myself.

*Poorvi Rajak*

# Acknowledgments

I extend my sincere gratitude to those who have played a pivotal role in the realization of this endeavor. Firstly, I would like to thank my parents from the bottom of my heart. They are like my backbone and always support me.

My sincere thanks to Professor V. Balamohandas for his continuous support.

I am really grateful to Jerome Bradley sir for writing the foreword.

My warmest thanks to Appala Reddy Y sir for his support and my wholehearted thanks to Dr. Srimathy Kesan ma'am for her invaluable message.

My heartfelt thanks to Mr. Sachin Chaturvedi, the founder of Anuragyam, for his constant support and guidance.

My deepest thanks to Dr. Joe K. Kizhakudan sir for his consistent support.

Last but not the least, I extend my grateful thanks to our school management and all my teachers for their continuous support and blessings.

*Poorvi Rajak*

Featured

India

# The Prodigy Artist: Poorvi Rajak, A Shining Star in the World of Art and Beyond

Poorvi's story is a beacon of inspiration for aspiring artists and individuals across the globe. Her achievements prove that age is no barrier to realizing one's dreams and that passion, coupled with determination, can lead to extraordinary accomplishments.

**Poorvi Rajak**
*International Book of Records Holder*
*A Student of Class 9 : Visakhapatnam, Andhra Pradesh*

# Poems

Photo Gallery

## New Year 2025

New Year is the time for new stories to begin
And for new skills and happiness to gain
A new canvas, it's time to take out
It is the time for a new plant to sprout

It is the time for new opportunities
Which come in great quantities
For new hopes, it is the time
It is the chance for life to reach its prime

So, go ahead and make the best
With your life filled with zest
This brand new year
Without having any fear

# To My Father

Papa, you are the light of my life
That always stays by my side
You are like a selfless tree
Sustaining us like the endless sea

Of endless love, you are a shower
You are tall and strong, like a tower
You are like a superhero
You protect me everywhere like a shadow

You deserve to be immortal
Because, your love is unnatural
You will always stay in my heart
Till eternity, we will never part

# Golden Justice

When we are in a difficult situation
And for a revolt, it is laying a foundation
When for justice, we decide to fight
When for change, a lamp we ignite

But sometimes, there is a factor of risk
Many people, from the fight they whisk
Due to the possibility of danger, out of fear
To prevent losing the feelings and things they hold dear

But we need to always remember
We must never surrender
Because in the fight for truth
Nothing will go smooth

Nothing, not even death, is a menace
When we fight for golden justice
It is a celebrated sacrifice, a contribution
For a just world, in the revolution

# Road of Life, the Stop of Success

In life, one thing you must remember
Then your success, no one can hinder
Giving up must never be in your mind,
Then success to you will be kind

On the road of life, there is a stop
From where, easy life you must drop
That is where after a long while
The stop of success will give you a smile

But the road of life is paved with difficulties
But you are stuffed with your abilities
They are hidden in the deepest corner of your soul
Which has no definite end, unlike a bowl

Dive deep and understand your strength
And on the road, go till the farthest length
Then you will meet extreme success
After a lot of rejections, hard work and distress

# I Can Work Alone

I feel so down
I know that I am not a clown
I'm in a tough situation
I have not searched for inspiration

For help I have not sought
Because I don't need to pout
Because I know what I can do
And for help, none I need to coo

Because I am independent
In my self-confidence, I have no dent
I am my own inspiration,
And can work alone, on my creations.

# Unheard Gossips

This one thing, I am not scared of
It's when people at me scoff
It's when people make fun of me
Many times that happening, I see

But, I am never let down
Even when I am portrayed as a clown
Because I know, I'm pure and true
And different is everyone's point of view

Remember, never get bothered
Of the gossips on you that are unheard
You are the one who knows your true self
So be unbothered, calm and by yourself

# Mahashivaratri

Salutations to the great lord
With your power everyone is awed
The one with three eyes
The place where power lies

O the world's first saint
The powerful Ganga, you restrained
The one with the crescent moon
The damaru, you dance to its tunes

Powerful demons, you defeated
Against halahala, us you guarded
Bless us with a good future and of hope, a ray
On Mahashivrati, this auspicious day

# What Makes Life Worth Living?

What makes life worth living
This question has left me grappling
With a sense of shock
My mind's peace has run amok

Is it the fact that we are rich?
Or that worldly pleasures we did ditch
Is it that you have a family to support
Or that we are living solitarily on a boat?

Is it that on people we used knives
Or that we have saved various lives?
Or that you have given life to someone
Or have lifted the spirits to everyone

Is it that to its fullest we are living every second
Our that someone's soul, you did torment
Or that someone for you is waiting,
Or that you, someone is dreading?

Is it that you are striving for world betterment
Or have achieved contentment
Or that we are living to someone's expectations
Or you are living every second in anticipation

All these 'or that's' will never end
My firmness to know the answer will never bend
The answer is now up to you
For thinkers like us are few.


The answers available are diverse
Creative, insightful or even adverse
Now to choose one answer,
My brain will have to re-suffer

## Women

A woman is a living goddess,
Whose presence removes darkness.
Women are behind the success of the globe
For development, they have endless scope

Women are constant role-shifters,
From dedicated leaders to brave fighters,
From naughty sisters to mothers who care,
And daughters who soar to activists who dare.

Let's salute the incredible women,
Whom skilfully, the society have woven.
For in every woman, a strength resides,
To build a future where justice presides.

# Holi

The celebrations for the arrival of spring
Melodies of music, around the place ring
Celebrations for the end of winter,
During this festival, everything is coloured

With colours and a smile, everyone is brightened
Everyone's cheerfulness and sprits are heightened
Enemies and strangers become friends
All types of cultures, now it blends

Tables covered with tantalising dishes
Social media filled with countless wishes
That is the magic of colourful Holi,
A celebration so divine, yet earthly

## Butterflies

After living as a tiny crawler
Slowly becoming bigger and bigger
Turning into a cocoon, eventually
Hoping to fly away, finally.

After spending months moulting
After it, through the cocoon cutting
After spending hours of toil
It once again, sees the Earth's soil

After the battle, extremely tiring
The world from above, admiring
It gracefully and courageously, takes into the air
To where it belongs, in the sky's lair

Now, it's one of the - Gentle creatures flying in the air
In the god's and fantasy's lair
Where otherworldly creatures reign supreme
At the place of every dreamer's dreams

Gentle creatures with resilient backgrounds
Frequent visitors of the flower-carpeted grounds
Helpers of the cycle of growth and renewal
One glance starts a journey, physical and spiritual

It is now, one of these winged angels

But those who face grave dangers

To save them we should try our best

To keep the earth full of zest

# Reopening of School

School is reopening soon,
And I am over the moon
It's the start of an academic year,
Which will create stories of glory and fear.

I am curious to know,
Which teachers in us will sow,
The seeds of goodwill and learning,
And tell stories which are inspiring.

I'm excited to learn new things,
Curiosity in me it springs,
Helping to know more of the world,
While in the classroom we are curled.

I can't wait to enter my classroom,
The place which takes away my boredom.
I can't wait to write another fresh story again,
Of the school year, which others consider mundane.

# Rama Navami

When on earth, there was darkness
And the virtuous were helpless
Lord Vishnu, on Earth he descended
In the form of Lord Rama, he incarnated

We celebrate the joyous occasion today
Of Lord Rama, coming to drive darkness away
May he bless us, to lead a fulfilling life
And for development on Earth, to strive

# Remember These Lines Below

When you are feeling bad
When in sadness you are clad
Whenever you are feeling low
Remember these lines below

I'm ever growing
To failure, I'm never bowing
I will never stop
To failure I'll never drop

When the tree's leaves have dried
When to sleep, yourself you have cred
When the bulb of despair will glow
Remember these lines below

Hope in the world is still left
It had never left
Keep growing non-stop
You will never stop

When you are ridiculed
Wrongly, you have been accused
When your life feels so low
Remember these lines below

I am the best, like me
That, I definitely see
I am like a bull in a china shop,
Breaking barriers I will never stop

Remember all the lines above
Into your brain, just shove
To make yourself invincible
Strong and unbeatable

# To My Mom

You are my precious lifeline
You are so kind and benign
You are my life's blossom
You are truly awesome

Like the blossom drenched tree,
Like the pristine blue sea
You offer me encouragement and solace
And never make me feel helpless

Life's forest, you help me navigate
With a fearless and steady gait
No matter how difficult it might be
Its positive side, you always see

You have made many sacrifices
To keep me away from darkness
Because of you my dreams take flight,
You have made my life so bright

Words fail but I know it is true,
That I am strong, because of you
Thank you for siding in my life's on going exam
And for making me what I am

# Save Trees

Trees, of life, the backbone
Endless creatures they have borne
For life on earth to sustain
And rid it of all its pain

Yes, the earth's pain they do rid
But what they got, with injustice it is filled
Humans cut them down, for their needs
But they cut down too much, to sustain their greed

Selfish, we all have been
And the consequences are being seen
And by all of us, is being felt,
Due to it, too much cruelty, the Earth has dealt

We can reduce Earth's burden
With trees, let's make it leaden
To restore the earth back to normal
And to make it immortal

We must definitely seek
To practise, not just preach
The earth will slowly recover,
A better earth, we will discover.

# Selfless Doctors

When our health is at the worst
Doctors are the people we seek first
When we feel our doom is near
They take us out of fear

They serve without partiality
Without caring about caste or nationality
During severe pandemics they fought back
They always had and will have our back

They need to be respected
To them we are ever indebted
Their dedication is boundless
For the lives they save are countless

They serve the people with endurance
And the universe thanks them with grace
They are the most worthy of respect
Because they make the world perfect

# Wind of Problems

Everything we've always enjoyed
Is going to be destroyed
By the incoming storm
In its invincible form

We can only aspire
In this situation dire
For the storm for us to spare
To face it, we don't have the dare

Everything we've always treasured
To shun, we'll be pressured
For a reasons, unexplainable
Happiness will be unattainable

Such is the storm's evil
It is the very devil
Prepare for the end
We are done for, my dear friend!

Everything we've always feared
All of them thave neared
We don't have any excuse
We have nothing to lose

If we have nothing of our own
Of what is this fear sown?
Why do we still cling on to 'fear',
When we know that the end's near?

A fire is weak if it always has a pout,
Loudly, it cannot shout,
When the storm nears,
The fire suddenly disappears!

But when a fire is strong and haughty,
And is extremely feisty,
The storm makes it fiercer,
Invincible and bolder.

## Fear

We all live here
Let's live without fear
Be it of any kind
Remember, it's all our mind

Fear wears us out
Gives us a pout
It anyways won't help
No matter how much you yelp

So it you just embrace
Without giving it a chase
For, you it helps to buckle
To face problems, with a chuckle

# Independence of India

We achieved independence 78 years ago,
And the seeds of a new India were sown
After 200 years of disdain,
With many warriors slain

People, with rage were seething,
Their blood was boiling
Over the atrocities committed,
Against them, whenever the Indians resisted

The people's rage was limitless
They were in distress
They fought valiantly
To bring back our glory

To remember our fallen heroes is our prime duty
They are the sacrifices behind our nation's beauty
To them, we must salute with immense admiration
We should look up to them in fascination

# Purpose of Life

The purpose of life will dawn on us someday
But when, we cannot say
Cause of life, it is one of the mysteries, profound
Who knows, when will it be found

It plagues my day and night
For its answer, it is indefinite
In the creases of the world it is hidden
But in my mind with this thought, every second is ridden

Without knowing its answer, why am I living?
Without knowing its answer, for what am I thriving?
And now one question leads to another
How oh how should I proceed further?

Without knowing its answer, at peace I'll be never
My every second of life, it's going to bother
With my minds thoughts, plagued I'll be
Eagerly waiting for the answer, only then I'll be free

# Ganesh Chaturthi

Lord Ganesh is the remover of obstacles
He helps us to reach pinnacles
Of the 'ganas', he is the leader
Of our lives, he is the caretaker

Today, let's celebrate his birth
For he makes sure that we are never hurt
Let's pray upon him for solace
And to bless the Earth with grace

Let's pray for world peace
And for prosperity on us to unleash
Let's pray for the world to be filled with cheer
And for togetherness and unity, sheer

# Father of the Nation

The revered father of our nation
The benefactor of the Indian population
Non-violence was his essence
Incomparable is his intelligence

He paved the way for our freedom
His movement was brave some
Of Non-cooperation movement, the leader
Of the Quit India movement, the spear header.

To us, he is an inspiration
Of a non-violent society, he laid the foundation
Let's adopt his ideals, for a future, better.
Of India's Bapu who is beloved forever

# One Day...It'll Happen

"You are a moron,
With dreams, forlorn
Your hopes, unrealistic,
Unattainable, with even a mystic

Heed my advice
To lead a life nice,
Abandon your aim,
For you are very lame"

People, will have said
But, you, say to yourself in your head,
That to lead your life, you are free
Unrequired is their decree.

"So you have your stead
But heed what I said
If not, your life, you'll ruin
Shattered, it'll be strewn"

The answer is nothing but silence, cold,
But, look at them with eyes bold,
And quietly work upon your aim
One day, success you will claim

Your answer will be your success
You'll achieve it, nevertheless
Their answer will be cold
Yet, more and more potential, you'll unfold

Eventually one day,
They'll come and say
What you'll never expect them to
What they say will shock you

"You're great, indeed
To you, I plead,
For us to please forgive
Us, you please believe

Sarcastic, I'm not being
From my heart, I'm saying
To you, I have been brute
 To you, I give a well-deserved salute"

This is imminent
If you work on your dreams with full intent
Ignore all the trolls
Fly high, achieve your goals

Do it, I know you can

To achieve it, day and night you might have ran

One day, success to you will greet

You'll realise, when your discouragers fall at your feet

# When You Fail to Meet Deadlines

You forgot to hand in the work which was due
Now you have nowhere to escape to
You are now in a hot soup
You are locked within a coup

You'll now be slaughtered
With the fire you'll be gutted
You're going to receive verbal lashes
Nothing of you will be left, not even ashes

The words are like blazing fire
The situation is really dire
Now you can't turn back,
You're tied within a sack

We are now powerless,
In front of the forces, ruthless
All we can do is to pray,
For our soul, in peace to lay!

But you have learnt a lesson, valuable
To compete your work in time you should be able
To give yourself an adrenalin rush
And to your procrastinating brain, give a shush

# Vijaya Dashami

The eventual good over immoral
That has been continuing since times immemorial
We'll be celebrating once more
In a celebration of happiness galore

After the battle which was fought fiercely,
This is the celebration, of Lord Rama over Ravana, the victory
Etched in the hearts and souls of the people
Who with day-to-day struggles, they grapple

## Shock the World

One day you will find
You can blow someone's mind
Everyone will be caught unawares
With your little but dramatic dares

You will drop a bombshell
In surprise, everyone will dwell
You'll knock them with a feather,
With surprise, they'll turn the colour of heather

You can do it with your talent
Which might be showcased or latent
Just the world, just unleash it
All at once or perhaps bit by bit?

# Captain CR Leena

Captain CR Leena is a significant inspiration for fearlessness,
She is the epitome of boldness
Of kindness, she was laden,
To receive the Sena medal, the first woman

On 16 July 1992, at 2 in the night,
They were moving, to run operations at another site
Then ambushed by anti-national elements
They were surprised by this development

The rain of bullets was ceaseless
Capt. CR Leena was fearless
To a person haemorrhaging, she gave instant first aid
To give aid, she was unafraid

Of the person, a life saved
To save him, bullets she braved
Let's pass her example to the next generation
To hold a stead in every situation

# Deepawali

Diwali, the festival of light
 Is a festival so bright
The harbinger of prosperity
Happiness and festivity

Though the essence is unchanged
Its demeanour has changed
It has become chaos over serenity
Due to crackers, a new amenity

Let's celebrate Diwali in an eco-friendly way
And send all negative energies away
Let's wish for a prosperous future
And for the world to prosper

# One In A Million

You are truly one in a million
Billion, trillion or zillion
In matters of person and books
And in matters of writing and being cooks

Our interests and hobbies
Opinions in designing lobbies
Various opinions we carry
Each greatly vary

Dressing style and sense
Whatsoever we reminiscence
Each and everything is different
But, this thing is barely apparent

It is high time, this we recognise
And uncover its clever disguise
Recognise each and every person's value
And give them respect, which is due

# What is Life ?

Life is complex
Anyone it'll perplex
Its twists and turns, it'll flex
Everyone it will vex

Everyone it will confuse
Leadings us to a short fuse
Sometimes, it will amuse
With life, we will never enter a truce!

Everything in life is iconic
As well as ironic
Everything is at its simplest
All well as complex, yet

Wait a second, what is life?
To know the answer we must strive
But some force, the answer away it will drive
To its conclusion, when will we arrive

Without its answer life how are we leading
This into wonder, me it is sending
Under its force, my mind's peace is dwindling
It will continue, till the answer is pending

From pending when will it come out?
Day and night with this question I pout
This question is like a rowdy bull, stout
Destruction to my mind's peace, it has wrought

My mind's peace, when will I get back?
It is troubling me like a tiny tack
Why is it hiding in a sack?
The answer, I will surely track

Days later, the answer is still hidden
With restlessness, my mind is ridden
This question, me will forever tease
My soul will never be at peace

# Freedom Held Back

An overwhelming sense of happiness
Of strength and boldness
Something felt after bravery
Or something felt rarely

Sometimes, inside us it is caged,
To be free, perhaps wars it raged
You might not have noticed it
Or to try to, you quit

Don't hold it back any longer
Got ahead and become stronger
We need to experience it, even some
For what you are holding back is freedom

# Ferocious Anger

A wave surges through
A feeling which we never knew, yet knew
So powerful, unrestrained
To hold it back, we've been trained

Makes you act uncontrollably
Make you react inconsolably
Gives you an Adrenalin rush
All of this out will gush

Let it, but in a safe way
If not so, who knows what happen May
Cause it is ferocious anger
In a wrong way, it can lead to danger

# Cold Disappointment

Your body is filled with numbness
Flushed out is your boldness
Staying still, yet restless
Just forever listless

Wondering if that's what you worked for
Shaken to the core
With emotions packed, for you, from rage to pity
Yet feeling so empty

But embrace yourself and move on
You are a force to reckon
For what you have felt was disappointment
It is cold and comes without and appointment

# Tomorrow

What is going to happen?
How is it shapen?
How am I going to feel?
Under what am I going to reel?

How is it going to unfold?
What surprises does it hold?
Whom am I going to meet?
What all am I going to eat?

These musings will never end,
Neither my curiosity will bend
Tomorrow, which comes every day,
Yet the one which never comes on any day.

# Soulful Rain

Here comes the music of nature
Something which can shape the near future
Something which various feelings can evoke
In the minds of city and town's folk

Here comes the nature's renewer
It's beauty is held in the eyes of the viewer
It washes everything anew
Exposing beauty, true

Here comes the nature's eternal force
Of daily lives, changing the course
Here comes the glistening rain
Harbinger of happiness or maybe pain

# Lights In The Night Sky

Lights in the night sky
Which never seem to die
Look like specks of dust
Covered in shiny, white must

Which twinkle against the darkness
Offering hope in bleakness
Forever sailors, guiding
With all people, forever siding

Groups of them sometimes form shapes
To look like animals, shapes or even grapes
Look at these tiny yet huge things in admiration
They are those stars which have sparked fascination

# A Peaceful Weapon

Magic you hold in your hands
The origin of bands
Something not to be taken lightly
A weapon, almighty

Of history it changed the course
Powers, it helped to reinforce
All, without bloodshed
While calmly sitting on the bed

The weapon is the humble pen
It can change the course yet again
All without any pain
Filled with happiness gain

# Unconquerable Ocean

Waves rushing back and forth
In the east and west, south and north
Crashing upon all surfaces
With its force of water, like maces

Ocean, the realm unconquerable
A force, incomparable
Spread across vast stretches of land
Crashing upon the sand

What mysteries does it hide
Beneath all that tide?
What is yet to be uncovered
In the depths, mystery covered

The giver of existence
Give and take is its essence
Yet we take too much, and give little
It unleashes its fury, on us, brittle

# Mystic Winter

When the days grow shorter
And the nights longer
When the sun is mild
When the Chills Smile

When warmth we seek
When days appear bleak
When with mist is shrouded
Around the hills, uncrowded

When some people make merry
When some celebrate gleefully
With colourful winter robes
Brighten the atmosphere, those

It is winter, gloomy
Yet in its own way, cheery
Another of god's creations, great
Something we ought to celebrate

# Beloved Motherland

Where we truly belong
Where peace and blissfulness throngs
Where to be we yearn
Were again and again we return

Were our soul is set free
Where we know every tree
Where our inner child
Is truly set wild

Where we want to stay forever
From where, leave we want to never
We grew up in this place's sand
For it is our beloved motherland

# Voice

We have a beautiful voice
That helps us to speak our choice
Voice can change the course
Of the world, for better or worse

A double edged weapon that is voice
It hurts more than a dangerous poise
Its impact can never be erased
For deep in the heart it is encased

Use this golden blessing wisely
Then you will be rewarded nicely
For all your positive impact
Given even without a pact

# Windowless Windows to The Past

Half hidden in soil
Excavated after toil
Perhaps can change the course
Of history, for better or worse

Windowless windows to the past
The ones to survive till the last
Once we uncover all the grime
They take us back in time

Something which is never anticipated
Something whose discovery is always celebrated
Fossils, the Windowless windows to the past
The ones to survive till the last

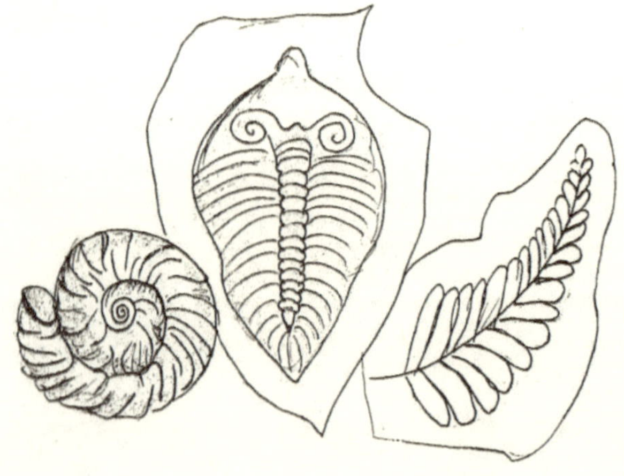

# Free the Never Freed

Many thoughts lie deep down
With a frown
Because they were never freed
Despite the need

They were never freed due to fear
Which would slowly come near
They were never freed and let out
Lest they make someone pout

They were never freed in minds curious
Lest they make someone furious
They were never freed even after being processed
Lest they make someone embarrassed

Free the never freed
You might do a splendid deed
Of with your thoughts, starting a revolution
For the good and the world watches in speculation

# Possessed by the Grasp of Determination

Something which pushes you
To do what you want to do
Never letting you stop
Or with exhaustion drop

Never letting you give up
Giving you adrenalin pump
Passing through all the poles
Of your set goals

Yourself you can manifest
By yourself you are impressed
Because you are now possessed
By the grasp of determination

# Those Forces

Beware of those forces
That force you to hold your horses
When on the way to success
They halt your progress

They come in clever disguises
Foolishness masked with wiseness
Set to break your hopes
And deter your scope

Just ignore these forces
And go through your own courses
They are mere distractions
From your goals, to create abstractions

# Renewed

In the abyss died down
Of despair and frown
All your ambitions
And your gleeful aspirations

Something happened perhaps
Leading you to sink in the gaps
As days pass, going deeper and deeper
And the climb up getting steeper and steeper

Remember that you just fell
Into a just a deep well
Do the thing which is right
Without any fright

Give it your hundred per cent
Begin the laborious ascent
This will never be repented
Because you are now renewed

# Worth For

How much am I worth for
From my tip to the core?
How much am I worth for Physically
As well as emotionally and mentally?

Am I even worth for?
Because everyone, me they ignore!
Fell totally invisible
Empty and miserable

Spew all that gloom
And your daily life resume
You know how much you are worth for
Unlock it and to the skies soar

# When You Have Lost

After everything you have lost
At every single cost
When you have lost the will
To continue even when the tides are still

When you have lost all hope
Unable to cope
Unable to bounce back
Lost all track

Fear not, it is not over
It will not be over forever
As long as there is this flame inside you
Your success is due

Go ahead and challenge your blues
And you will surely get good news
You will reach heights, stupendous
Of your success, tremendous

# Flame Inside Me

Whenever you are discouraged
You need to be encouraged
A mantra I will give
Your determination will live

There is a flame inside me
That everyone can see
It is bright and boiling
After years of toiling

No matter how hard you try
Inside it you will fry
Try to pour water
My flames everywhere will squatter

Try to throw sand
On your hand it will land
Not even baking soda is effective
Nor a fire extinguisher will hinder from its objective

My flame will never douse
It will always arouse
When you try to stamp it out
On your face it will leave a pout

Such is my fire

Such is its ire

Don't provoke it

It will engulf you, bit by bit

# Optimism

Why must we think about the bad
When it will make our mood sad
We must embrace hopefulness,
Optimism and cheerfulness

They lift our mood
Help us enjoy our food
Help us do things well
And positive things tell

This can make someone's day
And leave them in abandon gay
By just being cheery
You can make the world merry

# Control Anger

I am angry at something
Immense rage it brings
I can't cool down
On my face it has brought a frown

But, I need to control it
And I can control it, bit by bit
It is an important aspect of life
And will forever stay by our side

Anger is man's greatest enemy
It never allows us to think freely
It sends us in a spree
And makes us fume like a bee

## Positiveness

The world is full of negatives
We need to find the positives
They are floating everywhere
To follow them, we should dare

About positives we should care
As also share
Positiveness will make us happy
When we are gloomy

Accept and spread positiveness
And spread the brightness
All around the world
And a happier one we will have unfurled

# Technology

Technology is fascinating
The way it has developed is outstanding
Both the world around and itself
Also the cities and itself

It makes our lives comfortable
Its features are enjoyable
They keep us entertained
And our creativity unstrained

Let us appreciate
The things, which our burden alleviate
Let us develop it further
And our success, none can hinder

# Questions to Be Answered by Only You

Who am I?
What do I live by?
How am I?
Here, Why am I?

Such questions plague us
Tranquillity of our mind they snatch thus
We let others answer those
Answers, for us they choose

Only you can answer these
The real you, none sees
Only you know it truly
And can manifest it beautifully

# That Is the Law, That Nature Did Draw

Nature laid down a code
Of the way of life, it is an ode
For human nature, surprising
Sometimes supportive and demoralising

You might be small
But you can punch through a wall
That is the law
That nature did draw

You can be dangerous
When you are furious
That is the law
That nature did draw

You can be assertive
When the world is manipulative
That is the law
That nature did draw

Act upon the need's call
When troubles befall
That is the law
That nature did draw

# **Drowning**

Can't get out
Too much I have fought
To be free
I guess, I'll never truly be me

Trapped and drowning
It is overwhelming
Tears are spilling
From where is it starting?

Drowning in my fears
Drowning in my tears
Drowning in loneliness
Drowning in Lowliness

I'm trying to stay afloat
In this terrible moat
Surrounding my fort
Of my dreams the port

Swim across the tide
With you as your aide
You will conquer the fort
With your own support

# Supporters, Discouragers

There are people all around you
But those who support you are few
Many times with many people, it has happened
So don't get disheartened


Is might seem like everyone does supports
And with everyone, good is your rapport
But that is not the case
At every single little place


They are discouragers lurking
In the corners to discourage they are seeking
From various feelings, that desires stem
The fault is not yours, to get to you, don't let them

# Nervous Anticipation

When seconds feel like hours
When useless are our powers
Totally restless, you feel
Under the feeling, you reel

You can't wait, yet you have to
Nothing, you want to do
Your mind is etched with worry
With nowhere to bury

It is nervous anticipation
Of a turning point it is an indication
Embrace it like the good
Anything in life, you could have withstood

# Golden chance

When you see something golden
Hot as lava molten
To grab it, feeling like
Having an indecisive spike

It seems so tempting
Yet so threatening
To grab it is it safe
Or is it seemingly unsafe

Grab it before away it sails
If you don't want to hear your regretful wails
For this is a golden chance
Grab it, before out of your sight it will dance

## Just One More Step to Go

Just one more step to go
In this splendiferous show
Life is its title
Of this recital

Just one more step to go
In this blizzard of snow
To reach where you've always wanted to
After the difficult path passing through

Just one more step to go
In order to glow
Of success, in the light
Without any fright

Just one more step to go
In order to grow
In your existence
After all this persistence

Just one more step to go
Is all that is needed
To triumph and flourish
And your goal, to nourish

# The Last Straw

It is the last straw
And the line I draw
It is getting too much
The atrocity is such

I have beared it for long
Waiting for peace to throng
But I can't anymore
The hypocrisy is more

Don't hold it any longer
Why didn't you release it sooner?
Just raise your voice
Because it is your noble choice

# Sweet Taste of Victory

Ah, the sweet taste of victory
After hours of slavery
Is finally tasted
After the struggle, how long it lasted!

Your plans have been successfully fired
But now you are tired
After all, for so long you toiled
Lest the plans get foiled

Even now, don't rest
Refill yourself with zest
So long, you still have to go
Keep going on, so

# Unstoppable

I'm now unstoppable
My determination is unrestrainable
I'll never back down
Despite scornful frowns

I'm filled with power
I can fly taller than a tower
Because I am now unstoppable
My determination is unrestrainable

Keep going with this zeal
Your confidence you can feel
Your wounds you can heal
And the spotlight you can steal

## Carnival

The world is in harmony
Everything is a symphony
Everyone is filled with bliss
Nothing, anybody does miss

Celebratory music echoes around
The energy level is profound
Despair and sadness are kicked out
Everything's cheery, No one sports a pout

A period of celebration
Nobody is in isolation
Just bliss and glee multiplies
As the celebrations intensify

Of happiness, a unique time
As the festivity bells chime
Of every carnival
A time which is truly magical

# Waiting

After years of toil immense
Waiting with suspense
Will we have to wait longer
And be stronger?

We have been waiting eagerly
Since eternity
Heart's desire is going to be fulfilled
After the toil being tilled

Need to wait no longer
It is there in the front, yonder
A wave of calm and glee
Washes upon when you finally see

## Christmas

As the bells chime
We know it is time
For Christmas to celebrate
And for good mood to accommodate

Sent away are all the frights
As the trees are decorated with lights
In shades of green and red
Gloominess, this season, dreads

Legends of Santa Claus revolve
And children in making lists involve
This is the season of giving
And lots of merry-making

# I Lost the Battle

I lost the battle
Of my mettle
Confidence is crashed,
Hopes dashed

How should I proceed?
When will this despair recede?
I guess I am stuck like this
The good old times I miss

But, wait – left is the war
I have to fight for
Nothing other than myself
To the shouts of discouragement I am deaf

You might have lost the battle
But with your mettle
You will win the war
Now you are renewed than before

## A Revolt Long Supressed

When speak up the timid
When the revolt crosses its limit
Know that it was suppressed for long
And was waiting for the right gong

History has proved this already
While making the world peaceful and steady
To stop all the atrocities
And put an end to hypocrisy

When people are dormant for long
And of the last straw, the gong
Due to build-up
Of extreme pressure
The devastation is out of measure

# Joy

My adrenalin is high
I can touch the sky
I am unstoppable
And unrestrainable

Feeling so powerful
Feeling delightful
Got Goosebumps all over
Glad that the labour is all over

I would do anything to feel it again
Despite all its pain
It is unexplainable joy
It we should enjoy

# How the World Sees You

The way you speak
The way you sneak
The way a sigh of relief you heave
Is the way you achieve

The way you dress
The way you impress
The way you are moody
Shows the way you are truly

You only can depict yourself
And unite with oneself
Because that's how the world sees you
Your personality is few

# Windows to Our Souls

The feel in your eyes
Uncovers your disguise
Without any expressions
It opens multitude of emotions

No matter how hard you try
Not to show that you want to cry
Or any other emotion you want to hide
The compliance with your eyes will subside

For to the soul it is the window
Of the outside world, it is the inflow
But through it our true personality shines
Between the hidden and shown, it blurs the lines

# Imagination

In the world it is the best nation
It is imagination
Something which can never be defined
Nor can it be confined

It leads our mind astray
And brings us out of disarray
Into a world, totally another
Once, which none can ever bother

Embrace it with glee
For it makes you free
It is deeper than the sea
You might make something shocking, maybe?

# Racing Time

Time is flying
And we are left crying
In nostalgia of days of the past
Which are now in the mind's cast

Days are slipping faster
Turning into a disaster
We are now rushing
To keep in pace with timing

We have to keep up
With this racing time club
With our determination
We can pass this examination

Sovergein, Socialist, Secular,
Democratic, Republic
India
justice
liberty
equality
froternity
on
26
January
1950
to
26
January
2025
CONSTITUTION
of
INDIA
Glorious 75 Years

# Republic Day

Celebrating 75 years of our constitution
In the post-independence era, a revolution
In governing our nation
Which was in creation

Today is its celebration
Of hatred and boundaries an abolition
Reflection how far we have come
And thinking about what is yet to come

Where everyone unites
When nobody fights
When we are one as a nation
And everyone dances to the tune in coordination

As we resolve to develop
And prosperity envelope
We resolve to do it every year
For our nation, for us it is dear

# Poorvi Rajak Received Blessings

**A. Mallikarjuna, IAS**
(Former Collector of Visakhapatnam)

**Golagani Hari Venkata Kumari**
Mayor, Greater Visakhapatnam Municipal Corporation

**_M. V. V. Satyanarayana_**
Former Member of Parliament, Lok Sabha

**_Professor V. Balamohandas_**
Former Vice-Chancellor, Acharya Nagarjuna University

**Ed., Smt L. Chandrakala**
District Educational Officer, Visakhapatnam

**Velagapudi Ramakrishna Babu**
MLA, Visakhapatnam

**Mathukumilli Sribharat**
Member of Parliament, Lok Sabha

**Dr. Joe K. Kizhakudan**
Principal Scientist, ICAR CMFRI, Visakhapatnam

**Justice D. V. S. S. Somayajulu**
Visakhapatnam

*Hari Madala*
Founder, Book Magic Library, Visakhapatnam

**Book Presented to Visakhapatnam Public Library**

*Yogita, RJ at Radio City FM, Visakhapatnam*

***P.V.Mukund Rao*** (Environmental Engineer)
Andhra Pradesh Pollution Control Board,
Visakhapatnam

***Award Presented by Sachin Chaturvedi***
Founder, Anuragyam, New Delhi

# <u>More by the Author</u>

Available in :  amazon  

# Records & Awards Holder
(Poorvi Rajak, Visakhapatnam, Andhra Pradesh)

International Book of Records

Asia Book of Records

India Book of Records

India Proud Book of Records

Vande Mataram Award
Anuragyam, New Delhi

Bhartiya Baal Kala
Sanskriti Samman

www.ingramcontent.com/pod-product-compliance
Lightning Source LLC
Chambersburg PA
CBHW020600160726
47991CB00002B/800